Take Your Hat Off When The Flag Goes By!

A Child's Musical Introduction to the Constitution

Words and Music by
Janeen Brady

Illustrations
Evan Twede

Official product of the U.S. Jaycees and Schick®
Show Pride in America Promotion
– scholarships for America's youth.

ACKNOWLEDGMENTS

Orchestrated and conducted by Merrill Jenson
Engineered and mixed by Loren Ashcraft, Matthew Nickel,
and Bill Connor
Recorded at Bonneville Media Communications

© Copyright 1987 by Janeen Brady. All rights reserved. No part
of this book may be reproduced in any manner whatsoever
without written permission except in the case of
brief quotations embodied in critical articles and reviews.

Printed in the United States of America.

Dear Children,

It has been over 200 years since our great Constitution was written. Many people worked hard and sacrificed much to give us our priceless freedom. Since then many different generations have protected our freedom and passed it on to us.

Now it is our time to learn about America so we will be able to keep our nation free.

We at Brite Music hope this cassette and book will help you to more fully understand the values we Americans cherish so you will grow up to be the greatest Americans yet.

With love,

Janeen Brady

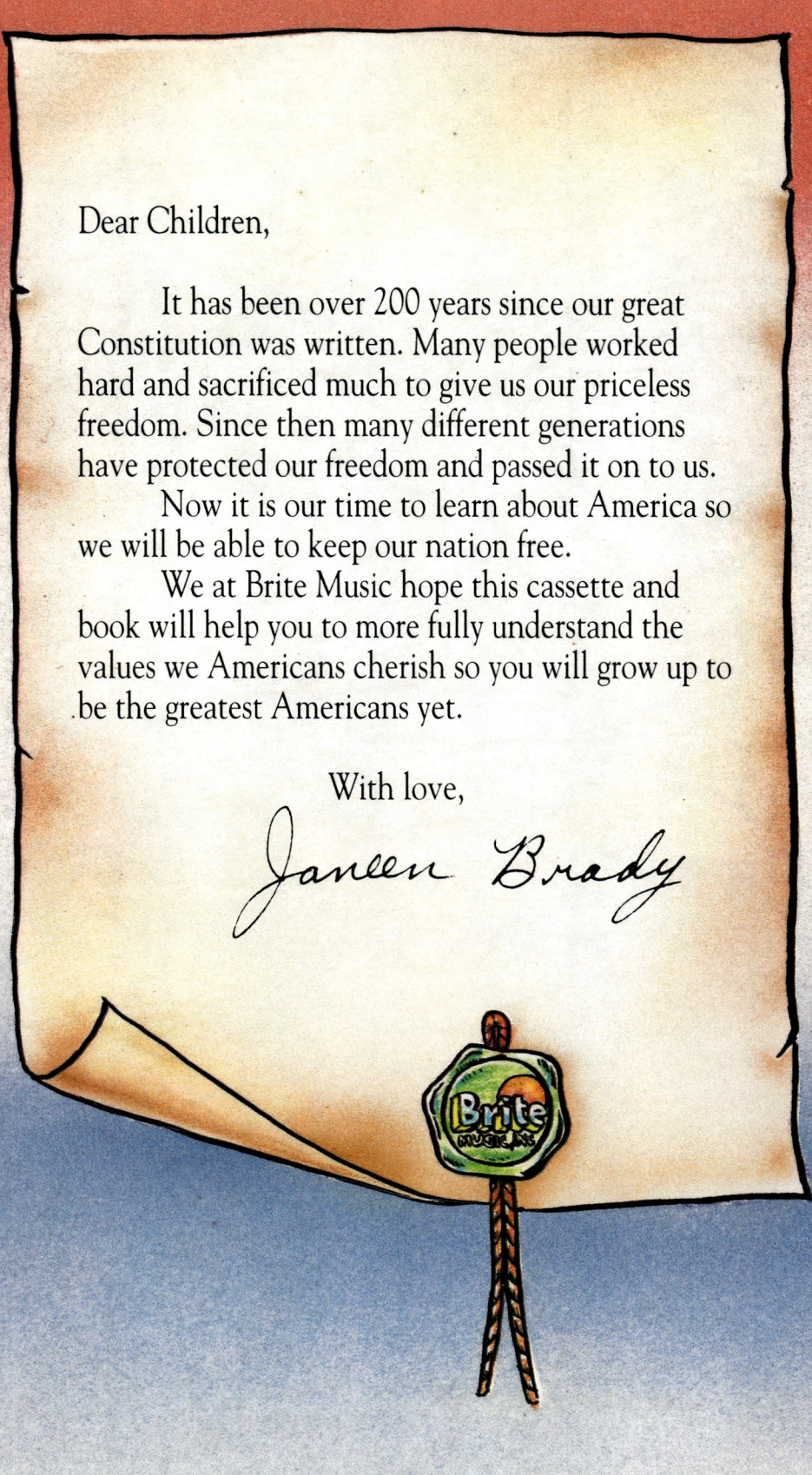

TAKE YOUR HAT OFF

Take your hat off when the flag goes by.
Get up and salute Old Glory waving there.
Take your hat off when the flag goes by.
You know that our flag's the grandest anywhere.

Can't you feel that good old tingling inside
When it's on parade?
Well, that's what we call Ameri-kind of pride, so don't be afraid

To take your hat off when the flag goes by.
Then throw out your chest and show the world you care.

I LOVE AMERICA

I love America, yes, I do.
I love America, love it true.
I love America, it's for me–
The home of the brave and the land of the free.

I love the ball games, I love the hot dogs,
I love the ice cream, love the sodas, too.
I love the fireworks, I love the bands,
I love the parades.
Yes, America, I love you.

I love America; it's my style.
I love America; see me smile.
I love America through and through,
The stars and the stripes and the red, white, and blue.

I love Manhattan, I love Grand Canyon,
I love Mount Rushmore, love the old bayou;
I love Niagara, I love Old Faithful, love
 Disneyland.
Yes, America, I love you.

I love America; hear me shout.
I love America; there's no doubt
I love America. Tell you why–
The feeling I get on the Fourth of July.

I love the mountains, I love the prairies,
I love the cities, love the country, too.
I love the rivers, I love the forests,
I love the oceans.
America, I love you.

In 1776

In seventeen seventy-six, my friend,
Americans were Englishmen,
But it was a miserable trick, a trick.
In seventeen seventy-six, you see,
We vowed to have our liberty,
For Parliament carried a stick, a stick.
In seventeen seventy-six, you know,
We said the king would have to go.
We didn't like his politics, politics.

He taxed us without representation.
Ruled us without authorization.
He limited our buying and selling
Till he forced us into rebelling.
The colonists kept trying to reason.
The Englishmen declared it was treason.

In seventeen seventy-six, we're told,
Such tyranny was getting old
And tension was terribly thick, was thick.
In seventeen seventy-six we dared,
And independence was declared,
And we got ourselves in a fix, a fix.
In seventeen seventy-six, my friend,
Old England's rule came to an end.
We showed them we wouldn't be licked, be licked.

GEORGE WASHINGTON

George Washington was a very good man,
A very good man, indeed.
He could have told a lie, but he said,
"Uh-uh,
The truth is what we need."
An honorable man, for his word was sure,
A man of great faith, for his heart was pure,
He was a very good, very good, very good,
Very good man, indeed.

George Washington was a very brave man,
A very brave man, indeed.
He could have stayed at home, but he said,
"Uh-uh,
A general's what we need."
He wouldn't give in to adversity.
His strength led his men on to victory.
He was a very brave, very brave, very brave,
Very brave man, indeed.

George Washington was a very wise man,
A very wise man, indeed.
He could have been the king, but he said, "Uh-uh, a king's not what we need."

He wouldn't be treated like royalty.
He wouldn't be called Your Majesty.
He was a very wise, very wise, very wise,
Very wise man, indeed.

MIRACLE IN PHILADELPHIA

It was nothing less than a miracle in Philadelphia
When our Constitution for this great land appeared.
It was nothing less than a miracle in Philadelphia
When our Founding Fathers assembled there that year.
Such different men, with different creeds,
Such different views and different needs,
Such new ideas and daring hopes,
Such thrilling words, the words they wrote,
That it was nothing less than a miracle in Philadelphia,
But its time had come, and democracy was here.

"If a sparrow cannot fall to the ground without God's notice, is it probable an empire can rise without His aid?"
–Benjamin Franklin.

"To suppose that any form of government will secure liberty or happiness without virtue in the people is a chimerical idea."
–James Madison.

"Our Constitution was made only for a moral and religious people. It is wholly inadequate to the government of any other."
–John Adams.

"America is great because she is good, and if America ever ceases to be good, America will cease to be great."
–Alexis deTocqueville.

CHECKS AND BALANCES

Now, the government works like a great, gigantic triangle.
No one holds all the power; that's made quite clear.
There are three branches of power in the great big triangle.
That's why a dictator never could make it here.
Checks and balances, checks and balances, checks and balances.

Now, one of the branches of power is the Executive.
That's the President of the United States,
The highest office in the land, you can be positive.
It's the President who administers affairs of state.

Now, another branch of power is the Legislative.
That is where they make the nation's laws.
The Senate and the House form the Legislative,
Americans all loyal to our cause.

Now, the other branch of power is the Judicial,
The highest court, Supreme in all the land.
That's where they interpret the laws and make them official.
Deciding what each law means, they take their stand.

Now, everybody checks on everybody else.
No one always gets his own way.
Yes, everybody checks on everybody else,
Keeping all the power in play.

WE THE PEOPLE

We the people of the United States,
In order to form a more perfect union,
Establish justice, insure domestic tranquility,
Provide for the common defense,
Promote the general welfare,
And secure the blessings of liberty
To ourselves and our posterity,
Do ordain and establish this Constitution
For the United States of America.

FALL APART

Everyone was hoping we'd fall apart.
We were young, and they hoped that we'd
    fall apart.
Wanting to get us in their grasp,
Never supposing we could last,
Everyone was hoping we'd fall apart.

England was hoping we'd fall apart.
We had wealth, so she hoped that we'd
    fall apart.
Wanting our taxes for her purse,
Wanting our riches even worse,
England was hoping we'd fall apart.

Indians on the warpath to the West,
Pirates attacking our ships; we couldn't rest.
The North and the South in a mad foray
And those in the middle, all in the way,
Colonies, each alone and under stress.

France and Spain were hoping we'd fall apart.
We were big, so they hoped that we'd
    fall apart.
Coveting how they could expand
If they could only own our land,
France and Spain were hoping we'd fall apart.

ESTABLISH JUSTICE

WHERE'S THE JUSTICE

If the cookie jar is empty
And you know you didn't take them,
But it's obvious somebody took the cookies
And they ate them,
And you fear that you'll be punished
And there's nothing you can do,
Remember what justice means to you.

'Cause where's the justice in, where's the justice in,
There's no justice in that.
If it's true you didn't take them,
But they still insist you ate them,
Ask for an investigation.
Justice gives you that.

If the schoolroom window shatters
'Cause a ball goes sailing through it,
And you're playing with your buddies
And you know you didn't do it,
But they tell you you're in trouble
And you're going to get it now,
Remember what justice means somehow.

'Cause where's the justice in, where's the justice in,
There's no justice in that.
If you know you didn't do it,
But they still insist you threw it,
Tell the truth and hold them to it.
Justice gives you that.

BIG WORDS

"Insure domestic tranquility."
Big words, big words.
What do they possibly mean to
    me?
Big words, those big words.
Grownups use words
    that I don't understand–
Strange to my ear but
    undoubtedly grand.
So I perform a quick word
    sleight-of-hand
And substitute words that I
    know.

Do you think that's quite apropos?
Why not? Hmm!

"Insure" means promise or
    guarantee.
Change those big words.
"Domestic" means home or
    community.
Explain those big words.

Last is "Tranquility."
Here's what it means:
Peaceful and quiet and calm
    and serene.
Now make the trade and
    we'll have a new scene
With substitute words in a
    row.

That's very clever, you know.
Thank you.

"Insure domestic tranquility."
New translation
Promises peaceful
    communities
In our nation.
Sheltered and quiet, safe
    from all riots,
Guarded from mobs at our
    schools and our jobs.
Turmoil must cease.
In America let us have peace.

Here in America you get to choose the work you do.
Anything you want to be is entirely up to you.
Many different kinds of jobs are waiting,
Each providing service or commodities
With a minimum of regulating,
Making this a great economy.
It's the secret of our industry.

LEMONADE 10 cents

Brown Eyes, Black Eyes

Brown eyes, black eyes, blue eyes, green eyes–
They all came to America.
Brown eyes, black eyes, like you've never seen eyes,
All the same to America.
Brown hair, black hair, braided down the back hair–
Many different kinds of people–
Red hair, blond hair, frizzy, straight, and long hair
Searching for a land that's peaceful.
Brown skin, black skin, red skin, white skin
All came here to America.
Brown skin, black skin, any skin's the right skin,

Each one dear to America.
Broad and brawny, tall and tough and tawny,
Big and swarthy, small and stout and hearty–
They all came to America.
They all came to America,
The melting pot of the world.
Irish, Spanish, Pakistanish–
They all came to America.
French and Russian, Greek and even Prussian–
All the same to America.
German, Swedish, English dressed in tweed-ish,
Many different kinds of people–

Japanese and even Polynesian
Searching for a land that's peaceful.
Folks from China, Italians so fina
All came here to America.
Mexicans and native Indians,
Each one dear to America,
Africans who didn't want to come
Now are glad they're each American.
They all came to America.
They all came to America,
The melting pot of the world.

SECURE THE BLESSINGS OF LIBERTY

FREEDOM OF SPEECH

ON THE AIR

AMERICA, I LOVE YOU

America, I love you, believe me, I do.
In my throat I feel a lump of pride.
America, I love you, believe me, it's true.
And when tears start welling up inside,
It's 'cause I love you,
Your goodness, your freedom, your light
You gave to me at such great cost.
America, America, I pledge to live my life
So not one precious freedom will be lost.

"God bless America,"
That's my America in that song.
"You're a grand old flag, you're a high-flying flag,"
And that flag's the flag I love; may it wave long.
Da, da, da da da, da da da,
And when I hear its music play
"America, America,"
Always makes me feel this way.

FREEDOM OF RELIGION

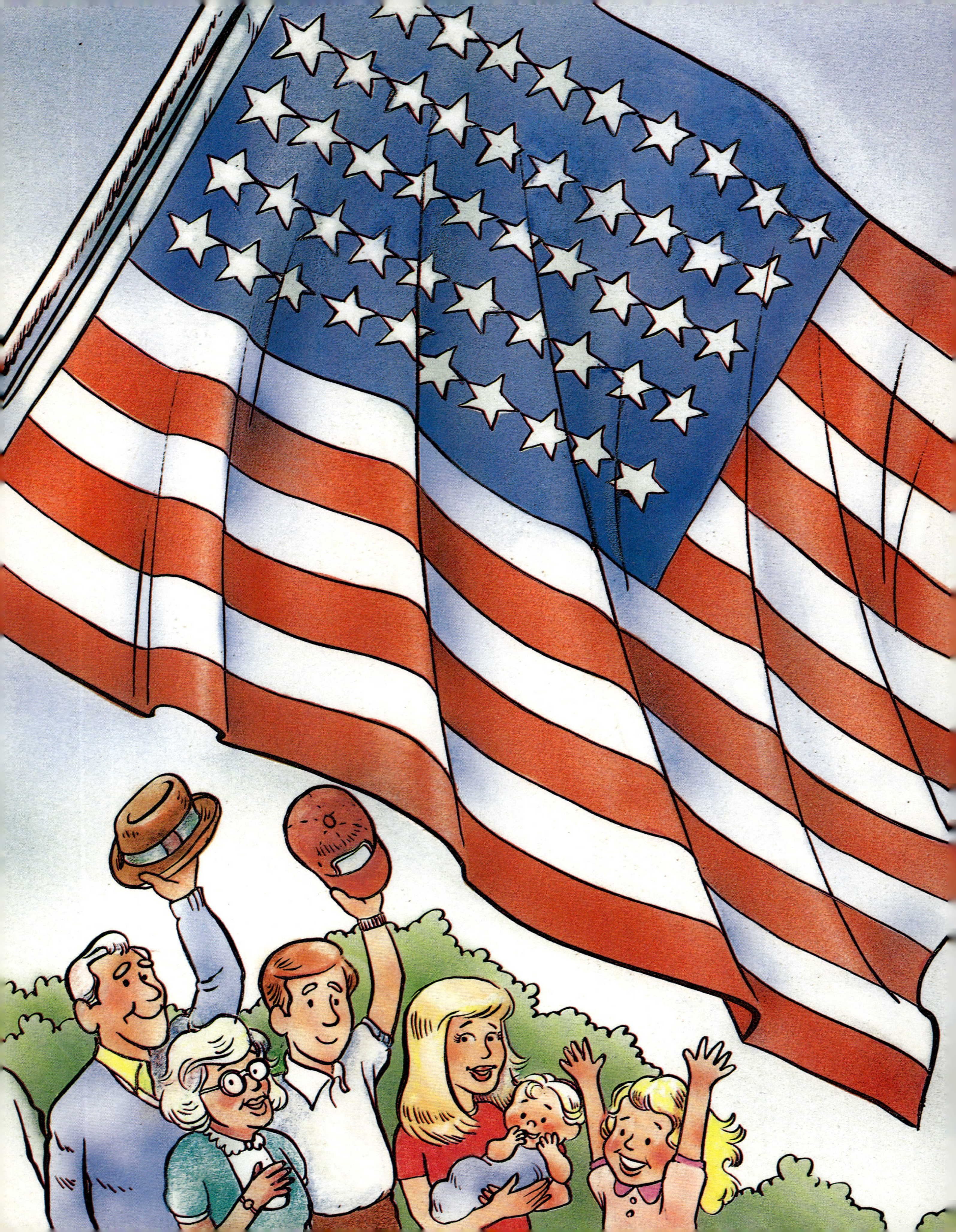

TAKE YOUR HAT OFF

Take your hat off when the flag goes by.
Get up and salute Old Glory waving there.
Take your hat off when the flag goes by.
You know that our flag's the grandest anywhere.
Can't you feel that good old tingling inside
When it's on parade?
Well, that's what we call Ameri-kind of pride,
So don't be afraid

To take your hat off when the flag goes by.
Then throw out your chest and
 show the world you care.

BASIC QUESTIONS ABOUT AMERICA

These pages are to be completed only after you have read the entire book and/or listened to the tape many times. Then you will be surprised how much you know.

1. What do we do when our flag goes by?
   _____

2. Our flag has three colors. They are ___ ___ ___ , ___ ___ ___ ___ ___ , and ___ ___ ___ ___ .

3. Another way to show respect for our flag is to put your ___ ___ ___ ___ over your ___ ___ ___ ___ ___ .

4. America was once ruled by the K ___ ___ ___ of E ___ ___ ___ ___ ___ ___ .

5. Name three things you love about America.
   1. _____
   2. _____
   3. _____

6. America rebelled against England in the year ___ ___ ___ ___ .

7. A patriot is someone who ___ ___ ___ ___ ___ his country and is ___ ___ ___ ___ ___ to it.

8. What did the patriots dream for and plan for and fight for? ___ ___ ___ ___ ___ ___ ___ .

9. Americans had many new ideas. One of them was: All ___ ___ ___ are created ___ ___ ___ ___ ___ .

10. That means ___ ___ ___ ___ ___ too.

11. What great patriot was our first president?
    ___ ___ ___ ___ ___ ___ ___ ___   ___ ___ ___ ___ ___ ___ ___ ___ ___ ___ .

12. What do we call the document which is the basis for our government?
    ___ ___ ___ ___   ___ ___ ___ ___ ___ ___ ___ ___ ___ ___ ___ ___ .

13. Our Constitution was written in the city of
    ___ ___ ___ ___ ___ ___ ___ ___ ___ ___ ___ ___ .

14. Because it was so hard to write, and because the government it established is so wonderful, many people called it a M ___ ___ ___ ___ ___ ___ ___ .

15. The __ __ __ __ __ __ rule in America.

16. Who is the servant of the people? __ __ __ __ __ __ __ __ __ __ __.

17. What do we call our unique system, which prevents any person from getting all the power?
__ __ __ __ __ __ and __ __ __ __ __ __ __ __.

18. The very first part of the Constitution is called the __ __ __ __ __ __ __ __.

19. How many promises are made to us in the Preamble? __ __ __.

20. All the states decided to become united. That is why we are called the
__ __ __ __ __ __ __ __ __ __ __ __ __ __.

21. Name the four branches of the military.
   1. __ __ __ __   3. __ __ __ __ __ __ __ __
   2. __ __ __ __ __   4. __ __ __ __ __ __ __ __

22. America does business based on the
__ __ __ __ __ __ __ __ __ __ __ __ __ system.

23. In America who chooses the kind of work we do?
_____

24. People came from many different countries to live in America. Can you name a country the people in your family came from?
_____

Is there another country other members of your family came from?
_____

25. Who are the only people who were already here when America began?
__ __ __ __ __ __ __. Sometimes they are called Native Americans.

26. The founding fathers believed a people can remain __ __ __ __ only if they remain
__ __ __ __.

ADVANCED QUESTIONS ABOUT AMERICA

1. Only one person was ever the king over America, and he was not an American. His name was _____ _____ the _____ , and he lived in _____ .

2. Name one thing the English rulers did that the colonists disliked.
   _____
   _____

3. What was the name of the document that Thomas Jefferson wrote?
   _____ of _____ .

4. The war the colonists fought with England to gain their freedom was called the _____ War.

5. "We hold these truths to be self-evident that all men (and women) are created equal." Where did these words come from?
   _____

6. We sometimes refer to George Washington as the _____ of our _____ .

7. What do we call the men who wrote our Constitution?
   _____ _____. Both words start with "F."

8. Name the three branches of power in the government E_____ L_____ and J_____ .

9. What two divisions of lawmakers make up the legislative branch?
   S_____ and H_____ .

10. Together they are called C_____ .

11. The President A __ __ __ __ __ __ __ __ affairs of S __ __ __ __ .

12. The Congress __ __ __ __ __ the nation's laws.

13. The Supreme Court __ __ __ __ __ __ __ __ __ __ the laws.

14. All of these branches of government are accountable to the __ __ __ __ __ __

15. Fill in the missing words:
    We the _____ of the _____ _____ in order to form a _____ _____ _____, establish _____, insure _____ _____, provide for the _____ _____ promote the _____ _____ and secure the _____ of _____ to ourselves and our _____ do _____ and _____ this _____ for the _____ _____ of _____

16. Name three countries that were hoping the American Colonies would fall apart.
    1. _____
    2. _____
    3. _____

17. Justice means that when a _____ is accused of a _____ that person has the right to a _____ _____, and he or she cannot be _____ until proven _____.

18. What does "insure domestic tranquility" mean?
    _____
    _____

19. In your experience, have we achieved domestic tranquility? _____

20. What do you think we could do to have more tranquility in our nation?
    _____
    _____
    _____
    _____

21. Why do we have a military? _____
_____
_____

22. The Free Enterprise system lets people reach for their __ __ __ __ __ __ .

23. Why did America get nicknamed "The Melting Pot"?
_____
_____

24. In America we are free to _____ where we choose; free to
_____ what we _____ ; free to _____ according
to our _____ .

25. Even though we didn't live 200 years ago, can we still be Patriots? _____

Note — There is no answer page for these questions. The answers are all found in the cassette program.